15593 EN
Sudanese Family, A

Archibald, Erika F.
ATOS BL 6.1
Points: 1.0   MG

A SUDANESE FAMILY

A SUDANESE FAMILY

By Erika F. Archibald

Lerner Publications Company • Minneapolis

The interviews for this book were conducted in 1994 and in 1995.

This book is available in two editions:
Library binding by Lerner Publications Company
Soft cover by First Avenue Editions
241 First Avenue North
Minneapolis, MN 55401
ISBN: 0-8225-3403-7 (lib. bdg.)
ISBN: 0-8225-9753-5 (pbk.)

Every effort has been made to secure reprint permissions. If an error has been made, please contact the publisher.

A pronunciation guide can be found on page 54.

LIBRARY OF CONGRESS CATALOGING-IN-PUBLICATION DATA

Archibald, Erika F.
    A Sudanese Family / by Erika F. Archibald
        p. cm. — (Journey between two worlds)
    Includes index.
    Summary: Relates the experiences of a family that came to the United States as refugees from a small farming village in the African country of Sudan.
    ISBN 0-8225-3403-7 (lib. bdg. : alk. paper)
    1. Sudanese American families—Georgia—Atlanta—Juvenile literature.
2. Refugees—Georgia—Atlanta—Juvenile literature. Refugees—Sudan—Juvenile literature. 4. Atlanta (Ga.)—Social life and customs—Juvenile literature. 5. Sudanese Americans—Georgia—Atlanta—Social life and customs—Juvenile literature. [1. Sudanese Americans. 2. Refugees.] I. Title. II. Series.
F294.A89S773 1996
975.8'231004927624—dc20   95–39841

Manufactured in the United States of America
1 2 3 4 5 6 – SP – 02 01 00 99 98 97

This book is dedicated to Dei Jock Dei.

(Above) *For nearly two decades, a civil war has torn this Sudanese woman's homeland apart. Many people are forced to leave the country because their villages have been demolished. Refugee camps like this one* (facing page) *provide shelter and relief to families on the run, but refugees face other problems such as overcrowded conditions and severe food shortages.*

SERIES INTRODUCTION

What they have left behind is sometimes a living nightmare of war and hunger that most Americans can hardly begin to imagine. As refugees set out to start a new life in another country, they are torn by many feelings. They may wish they didn't have to leave their homeland. They may fear giving up the only life they have ever known. Many may also feel excitement and hope as they struggle to build a better life in a new country.

People who move from one place to another are called migrants. Two types of migrants are immigrants and refugees. Immigrants choose to leave their homelands, usually to improve their standards of living. They may be leaving behind poverty, famine (hunger), or a failing economy. They may be pursuing a better job or reuniting with family members.

Refugees, on the other hand, often have no choice but to flee their homeland to protect their own personal safety. How could anyone be in so much danger?

Traditional lifestyles are threatened in Sudan.

The government of his or her country is either unable or unwilling to protect its citizens from persecution, or cruel treatment. In many cases, the government is actually the cause of the persecution. Government leaders or another group within the country may be persecuting anyone of a certain race, religion, or ethnic background. Or they may persecute those who belong to a particular social group or who hold political opinions that are not accepted by the government.

From the 1950s through the mid-1970s, the number of refugees worldwide held steady at between 1.5 and 2.5 million. The number began to rise sharply in 1976. By the mid-1990s, it approached 20 million. These figures do not include people who are fleeing disasters such as famine (estimated to be at least 10 million). Nor do they include those who are forced to leave their homes but stay within their own countries (about 27 million).

As this rise in refugees and other migrants continues, countries that have long welcomed newcomers are beginning to close their doors. Some U.S. citizens question whether the United States should accept refugees when it cannot even meet the needs of all its own people. On the other hand, experts point out that the number of refugees is small—less than 20 percent of all migrants worldwide—so refugees really don't have a very big impact on the nation. Still others suggest that the tide of refugees could be slowed through greater efforts to address the problems that force people to flee. There are no easy answers in this ongoing debate.

This book is one in a series called *Journey Between Two Worlds,* which looks at the lives of refugee families—their difficulties and triumphs. Each book describes the journey of a family from their homeland to the United States and how they adjust to a new life in America while still preserving traditions from their homeland. The series makes no attempt to join the debate about refugees. Instead, *Journey Between Two Worlds* hopes to give readers a better understanding of the daily struggles and joys of a refugee family.

Families try to produce enough food to survive from the dry soil of northern Sudan.

The long journey to the United States for nine-year-old Dei Jock Dei began in Kenya, East Africa, on a hot June day in 1994. Early that morning, his family gathered their few belongings and took a bus from the harsh, desert refugee camp. With 40,000 people living in tents and makeshift huts, the camp was not home. But then Dei had not known a real home for most of his short life.

Years earlier, as a very young child, Dei had left his homeland of Sudan because of civil war. He had traveled by foot with his mother, Nyawal, to refugee camps in nearby Ethiopia and Kenya. These camps offered food and safety to the people of Sudan whose villages had been destroyed by the fighting. At the same time, Dei's father, Jock, had parted from the family to seek an education at missionary, or religious, schools in Egypt—a nearby country in northeastern Africa.

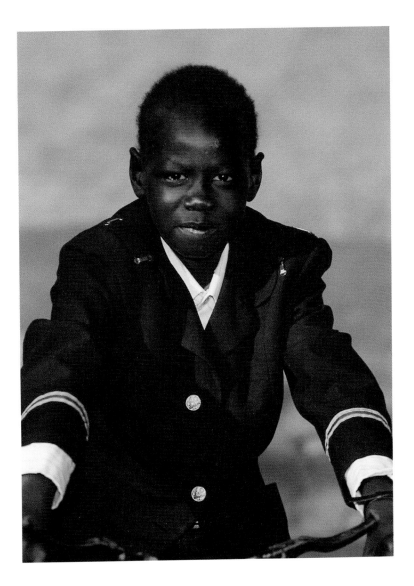

Dei Jock Dei adjusts to life in the United States. His family migrated from Sudan in order to escape the violence they faced in their own country.

After years of separation and hardship, the family was reunited and received permission to come to the United States in search of a safe home and a peaceful life. They set out on a very tiring airplane journey that began in Nairobi, Kenya, and ended several days later in Atlanta, Georgia.

"Long and bumpy" is how Dei remembers the trip. Along the way, his family stopped in Amsterdam, the Netherlands, to change airplanes. In New York, U.S. customs agents checked the family's official papers, allowing them to enter the country.

Finally, they arrived in Atlanta, at five in the morning. Dei's father walked off the plane first, dressed in a suit that looked something like a military uniform. Dei followed, along with his mother, who was holding his little brother Pal. Dei's aunt Nyachan—his mother's teenage sister—also came with the family.

"They weren't hard to spot," says Tom Bryant, a member of a church group in Atlanta that sponsored

(From left to right) *Jock, Nyawal, Pal, Dei, and Nyachan stand in front of their first apartment in the United States. They've had to learn many new things since their arrival.*

The skyline of Atlanta, Georgia, was one of the first sights for the newcomers.

the family. He and Phil Bader, another church member, greeted the family. "We had no photos of them, and we didn't know if the family spoke English. But we had no trouble recognizing them as they got off the plane. They were looking lost and exhausted."

As it turned out, Jock spoke some English. The others did not. The hosts welcomed the family to the United States with handshakes, smiles, and a few balloons. Because the plane got in so much later than originally planned, a welcoming celebration set up by the church had been canceled. Leaving the huge, modern Atlanta airport that early morning was the first of many new experiences for the family. Nyachan was frightened by the long airport escalators, so Tom demonstrated by getting on the moving stairs first. Dei followed close behind.

Airplanes and escalators were quickly followed by computers, bicycles, grocery stores, and even snow. Dei soon decided that he didn't like cold weather. But bicycles, computers, cars, orange soda, and hamburgers—well, those are great!

The stark contrast of the desert (top) *to the fertile river valley* (above) *reflects the vastly different landscapes that exist in Sudan.*

 Sudan is the largest country in Africa. The nation lies in the northeastern part of the continent. Its neighbors are Egypt to the north; Eritrea and Ethiopia to the east; Kenya, Uganda, and Zaire to the south; and the Central African Republic, Chad, and Libya to the west. Northern and southern Sudan—and the people who live in the two regions—differ from one another in many important ways. These differences account for many of the troubles the country faces.

Northern Sudan consists of desert lands crossed by the Nile, the world's longest river. The majority of people in this region live alongside the river. Most are of Arab descent and follow the religion of Islam. They believe in one God (called Allah) and in his prophet Muhammad, who founded the religion in the A.D. 600s.

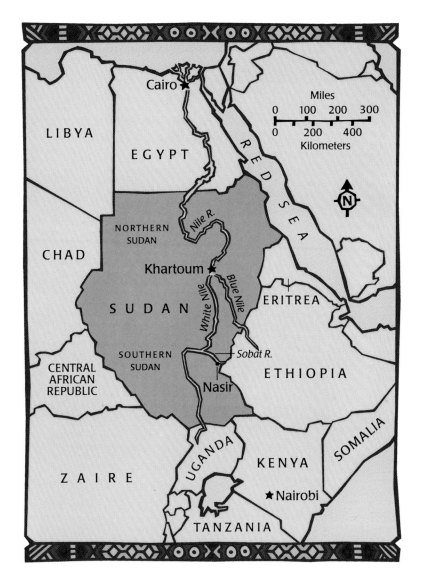

Jock and his wife Nyawal moved from their village near Nasir to Khartoum before Dei was born. Dei has spent much of his life moving from place to place.

NUER LIFE

Dei Jock Dei's family is from a small village on the Sobat River in southeastern Sudan. The region's many waterways feed the great Nile River as it makes its way northward. Unlike the north, southern Sudan is fertile, and crops grow well.

"The place where we come from is near a small town called Nasir," Jock explains. "The land is very flat, and most families are farmers. Also, we do fishing in many rivers and raise cattle, goats, and sheep."

Many young Nuer men travel with grazing cattle. "We have permanent houses, but the young men take the cattle and graze far from home with them. We build shelters to stay in then," Jock says.

Cattle are immensely important to the Nuer. These animals are the pride of the tribe and figure prominently in many aspects of Nuer life. In the United States, however, Jock will not be able to find work doing traditional Nuer labor. He and other Sudanese refugees must develop new job skills and look for different kinds of work.

The people in southern Sudan are black Africans, and most are not Muslims, or followers of Islam. Although the area is home to many ethnic groups, the majority of people are Nilote. This group is divided into smaller groups, called tribes. Each tribe has its own culture and religion, and its members have their own unique way of living.

Dei's family comes from a large Nilotic group called the Nuer people. The Nuer are farmers, who rely mainly on herding cattle, but also raise goats, sheep, millet (a type of grain), and maize (corn). The Nuer are known for being very tall and for decorating their faces with special markings that form small, round scars.

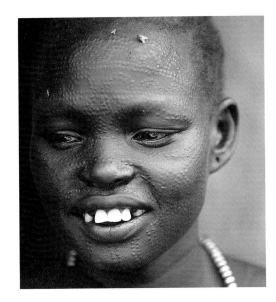

(Top) *This Nuer woman has customary round markings on her face. Nuer men have six additional long, horizontal scars on their foreheads.*
(Right) *Markets like this one in western Sudan are less common in the southern regions of the country.*

The government of Sudan is run according to Islamic beliefs and laws, which apply to all Sudanese citizens, regardless of their religion. Life is difficult for non-Muslim citizens, such as the Nuer people and their neighbors in the south.

Many historical forces have shaped the current government of Sudan. For thousands of years, people have lived along the Nile. By about 2000 B.C., a number of small states existed along the river in Nubia, an area in the northern part of what is now Sudan. Egyptians soon began to influence their neighbors in Nubia and at times ruled over the region.

Nubia later came under the influence of the Roman Empire, which spread throughout much of Europe, western Asia, and North Africa. By the A.D. 500s, the Eastern Roman (or Byzantine) Empire had sent leaders to Nubia to teach the people there about Christianity. Christianity is based on the teachings of Jesus and a belief that there is only one God.

About 100 years later, Arabs conquered Egypt. These invaders, who were Muslims, came from an area in southwestern Asia called Arabia. By the 1500s, Arabs controlled northern Sudan as well. Eventually, most of the people in the region intermixed with the newcomers and adopted Arab culture and the Muslim religion. They considered themselves to be Arab.

At the same time, black African groups were living in southern Sudan. The Nuer and the Dinka peoples were among the black Africans. These people had no contact with Arab culture. They had their own ethnic backgrounds, languages, cultural traditions, and religions.

By the 1800s, Muslim leaders in Egypt had gained power in Sudan. In 1882, Egypt came under the control of Britain. During the late 1800s, Egypt and Britain together ruled Sudan. Many Sudanese people protested. Some wanted Sudan to be independent. Others wanted to return to traditional Egyptian rule. After many uprisings in Sudan, Britain and Egypt decided Sudan could govern itself. Sudan officially became an independent nation in 1956.

Arab culture influenced northern Sudan. This medieval door stands near the Red Sea.

But independence did not end problems for the Sudanese people. Southern Sudanese citizens feared that the northerners would take over Sudan and force them to convert to Islam. Since independence, northern and southern Sudan have been at war almost constantly. This civil war, which is fought mostly in the south, has disrupted farming. Unable to raise food, many people have gone hungry. Drought (a severe lack of rain) sometimes makes the food shortage even worse. Famine conditions are a part of life in the south.

This village was destroyed as a result of the civil war raging in Sudan. Hundreds of thousands of people have been forced to leave their homes.

(Left) *Khartoum, the capital of Sudan, is situated in the northern part of the country.* (Below) *Students work very hard. The government offers six years of primary school education taught in Arabic. In the north are upper level schools, which few non-Muslim students are allowed to attend.*

 Dei's father and mother left their war-torn village in southern Sudan not long after they were married. They went to Khartoum, Sudan's capital city in the north, where Dei's father studied at a missionary school.

"We first left Nasir, where I was born, in 1985," Jock explains. "I was not allowed to get an education. I started to study at primary school, but then the war closed down the school. I requested to go to another school in the north, but the government refused."

Dei's father had decided as a young man to convert to Christianity. He became a member of the Seventh Day Adventist Church, which believes in the return— or second coming—of Jesus. The church helped Dei's father go to high school and get some college education. This accomplishment is rare for a southerner. The Sudanese government usually does not allow non-Muslims to attend upper-level public schools.

Jock left Khartoum to pursue his education in Cairo, Egypt (left), while Dei and his mother fled to safety in a refugee camp like this one in Ethiopia (bottom).

Dei was born in 1985 while his parents were living in Khartoum, where the persecution of non-Muslim residents was sometimes very harsh. To avoid this threat, the young family decided to leave the capital. Jock went to another missionary school in Cairo, Egypt. Dei and his mother went back to their village in the south. But the civil war made living there unsafe. Like many other people from southern Sudan, Dei and Nyawal fled to neighboring Ethiopia in 1987. The Ethiopian government welcomed them, along with many other Sudanese people, into large refugee camps.

The Ethiopian camps housed thousands of homeless people from southern Sudan in tents and huts. Usually the refugees got along well. But fighting would sometimes break out among the different groups at the camp, because there wasn't much else for them to do.

In 1991, after Dei and his mother had spent several years in the camp, the Ethiopian government closed the refugee camps and forced the Sudanese refugees to return to Sudan. Because life was so dangerous at home in Nasir, Dei and his mother kept moving. That same year, Jock left school in Cairo to search for his family. He traveled to Kenya, where many of the refugees who had lived in Ethiopia had moved. After about a year, the Red Cross (an international aid organization) located Dei and Nyawal and reunited them with Jock.

"We were separated for five years," says Jock about the family's time apart. "It was very hard, very difficult."

Jock still wanted to finish his schooling. He found a missionary college in Tanzania, another East African country, and the family moved there. Dei's younger brother Pal was born in 1992, while the family lived in Tanzania. Dei had his first opportunity to attend school. He began to learn a new African language called Swahili. Dei also remembers seeing his first television and refrigerator at this time.

During the family's stay in Tanzania, Dei's father decided the family should leave Africa altogether and come to the United States. "I'd wanted to come to America for a long time," Jock says. But after suffering the scare of not being able to find his family in Kenya, he knew it was time to act. To make the move, the family contacted the United Nations (UN). This international organization helps people in troubled and war-torn countries.

A CARE worker hands out food to hungry children. CARE (Cooperative for American Relief Everywhere) provides food, health care, and emergency assistance to refugees around the world.

Dei's family spent several months in a refugee camp in Kenya while waiting for the UN to grant them official refugee status. Dei's last memories of Africa are of the camp's building styles (above and left), *and the many wild animals that roamed nearby* (facing page).

Dei's family applied to the UN for official refugee status, which would allow them to move to the United States. This process takes a long time because there are many applications from around the world each year. Before making a decision, the UN must first determine whether families will be in danger if they return to their homelands.

In 1994 Dei's family, along with his aunt Nyachan, moved to a special UN refugee camp in Kenya to wait for final approval. This large camp is the part of Africa Dei remembers most. He recalls that families lived in tents or in mud-and-stick huts with thatched roofs they built themselves. Water taps brought fresh water from underground wells. Some families tried to grow extra food in small gardens. Refugees also constructed giant outdoor churches for worship services. Dei also recalls thorn trees, riverbeds filled with sand, and many wild animals. Mainly, though, he remembers how hot and dusty the camp was and how difficult it was to keep clean.

Finally, in the summer of 1994, the UN approved the family's official refugee status. A U.S. immigration agency called the Immigration and Naturalization Service gave the family medical checkups. If they had not passed this final check, they would not have been allowed to leave. "It was very lucky. We were all healthy," says Jock.

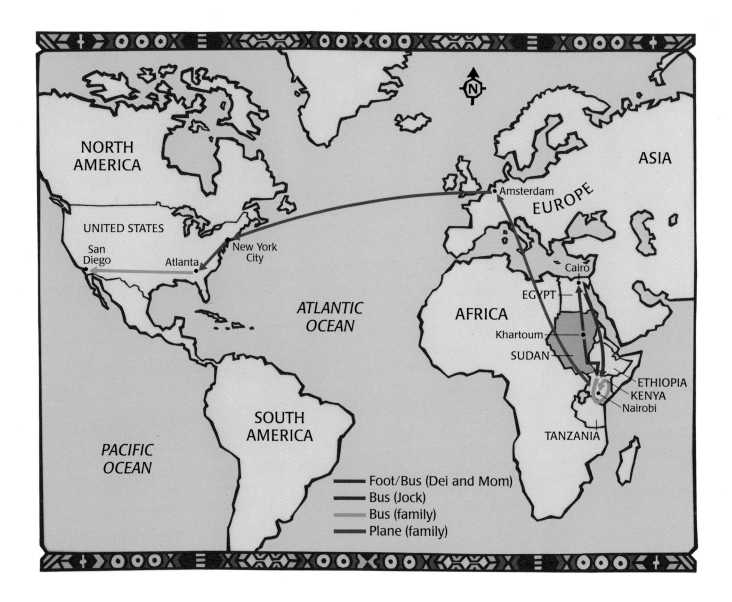

 With no money and few belongings, Dei's family needed help to settle in the United States. The organization that helped them was a Christian agency called World Relief.

World Relief tries to place refugees from one country together in the same city so they can be near others who speak the same language and share similar cultural traditions. These communities help ease the transition to life in the United States. For Dei's family, World Relief chose Atlanta because another Sudanese family had recently settled there. Atlanta's Westminster Presbyterian Church, whose members wanted to help a family in need, was available to act as a sponsor.

Members of Westminster Presbyterian Church in Atlanta, Georgia (left), *helped Dei and his family adjust to their new home. Attaining this document* (above) *was the first step in the family's long journey to the United States.*

This is the family's first home in their new country.

As the sponsor, the church agreed to take responsibility for Dei's family for three months. This arrangement included paying for rent, food, and other daily living expenses. Families from the church formed committees to find an apartment for the family and to collect donations of furniture, bedding, kitchen utensils, and clothing so Dei's family could quickly settle into their new home when they arrived.

Church members also stocked the kitchen with milk, bread, fruits, and vegetables. They didn't know exactly what the family liked to eat, so they decided not to buy any packaged or ready-made food that the family might not use.

Although everyone was exhausted from the long trip, Dei's father wanted to learn about the apartment right away—especially how to use the lock and keys and how to turn off the air conditioning, which the family was not accustomed to using.

Within the first few days of the family's arrival, church members took them to a grocery store. This was Dei's first experience of plentiful food. At the refugee camps, each family received only basic rations of grains, oil, a little bit of fish or meat, and vegetables. There wasn't always enough food for young, growing children. In fact, when Dei arrived in Atlanta, he was beginning to show signs of malnourishment, a condition that happens when people don't get enough food to grow properly and to remain healthy.

The staple food of the Nuer people in Sudan is millet. Called *dra* in the Nuer language, millet is a type of grain. A typical meal in the family's homeland would include dra, chicken or fish with spices, green vegetables, and milk. In the United States, their meals often consisted of white rice with bits of chicken and salsa (a tomato sauce).

Dra, *or millet (top),* was an important part of the family's diet in Sudan. Nyawal (right) *has had to learn to cook with new foods bought in stores in the United States.*

Church members showed Dei's parents how to work the stove, refrigerator, and vacuum cleaner. The sponsors also taught them how to use public transportation, including city buses and the subway. Jock asked many questions. He was interested in learning how businesses operate in the United States so that he could look for a job. Jock also asked for maps of the world and of the United States. The family studied these to learn exactly where they were living.

"Jock was very inquisitive, like a sponge," says Tom Bryant. "He also wanted to tell us about the situation in Sudan and the people he left there."

"Our sponsors are good people," comments Jock. "They do it all for love."

In his bedroom, Dei has a map of the world, on which he can see just how far he has come.

Dei's parents have had many new situations to deal with all at once. Their Atlanta neighborhood is quite diverse, with many other immigrants and ethnic groups living nearby. The apartment itself has a living room, two small bedrooms, and a tiny kitchen. Dei's room is furnished with two bunk beds and a single bed. He, two-year-old Pal, and Nyachan share the room. On the wall, there is a large map of the world.

The neighborhood has some crime and violence, and at first the family was unsure how safe it was for Dei and the other youngsters to play outside. Sometimes police cars would arrive in the parking lot outside the apartment complex because of reports of violence in the area. Dei's family would watch the flashing lights from their windows. Although the family survived a war in Sudan, they worry about a different kind of violence in the United States.

Jock notes, "In Africa you see war and you run from it. Here it is everywhere. Africa may be better in this way. You can't get away from the violence here."

Dei stands with friend, Kong, a Sudanese boy who lives upstairs.

Because the family moved to Atlanta during summer vacation, Dei could not start school right away. He spent many of his first days in the city sitting on a chair outside the apartment. He also played with his new friend, 13-year-old Kong. Kong and his family are also from Sudan, and they live upstairs.

Dei had seen a television before, but in Atlanta he was introduced to American TV programs. At first he knew very little English but could laugh along with the action. Dei's father is unhappy about the kinds of shows Dei sees on TV. He feels there is too much violence, noise, and nonsense.

"TV is okay for news," he says, "but I don't like it. We need to read and to study the Bible."

When asked why he watches television, Dei answers quietly, "Because I like it."

Dei and his family wear American clothes donated by Westminster Church rather than traditional Sudanese clothing. Like other Nuer people, the family members are very tall. At nine years old, Dei is already about five feet (1.5 meters) tall. His mother and father

Among other things, Dei enjoys watching television in his free time.

The hotel in Atlanta where Jock first found work

are both well over six feet (1.8 meters) tall, and 15-year-old Nyachan is approaching six feet as well. Jock says he is one of the shorter members of his tribe.

One of the most important things Dei's father did when he arrived in Atlanta was to look for a job. Although he had taken some college courses in Sudan, Jock knew he would not be able to get a high-level job in the United States without more training and better English skills. And without a car, he needed a job he could get to by bus or train. World Relief and the Westminster Church helped Jock look for work, but he found a job on his own—working in the kitchen of a large luxury hotel in Atlanta.

The job was during the nighttime. This schedule was very hard, because Jock slept during the day and didn't get to spend time with his family. Jock made just enough money to pay rent and buy a little bit of food. He didn't know how he would pay for other necessities, such as electricity and clothing, and he worried about how he would support his family.

After several months working in the hotel kitchen, Jock found a different job, cleaning airplanes at the airport. This job required him to work at night as well, keeping him away from the family. As with the hotel job, it did not pay enough to support them.

"I don't know what we will do," he worries frequently. "It is very hard."

*The night skyline of busy
downtown Atlanta, Georgia*

Classrooms like this one in the south were a rare sight during the civil war in Sudan.

 Dei's life in the United States improved once the school year began. Although he was nine years old, Dei enrolled in second grade, because he hadn't been to school much in the past and did not yet speak English. Woodward Elementary, his school in Atlanta, is very close to the apartment. Dei walks there with his friend Kong.

Dei enjoys learning, and school is the focus of his life. He has learned some English but is shy about speaking. Dei is impressed with the large, modern school and with all of its equipment. Desks, computers, and lots of books surround Dei in his classroom in Atlanta.

What does he remember about his school in Africa? "He remembers the school in the refugee camp in Kenya," says his father, translating for Dei, who speaks in the Nuer language. "The children sat on the ground in dirty clothes."

While Dei prefers the tidiness of Woodward Elementary, he misses the wild animals he saw near his school in Kenya. Buffalo, elephants, hyenas, and giraffes could be seen from his classroom. "Sometimes the buffalo came and knocked people down," he recalls.

Dei's class at Woodward Elementary has about 20 students, including some from countries such as Mexico and Ukraine. At school the teachers and students call him "Dei Dei," because his name mistakenly was listed as Dei Dei Jock, instead of Dei Jock Dei. Since several other students are also learning English for the first time, they all go to a special classroom in a trailer next to the school building, where they practice speaking the language for part of the day.

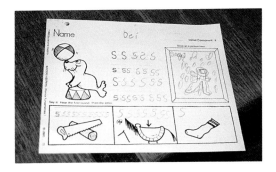

Dei learns how to read and write English. In one exercise (top) *he learns to write the letter S.* (Right) *The other children in his ESL (English as a Second Language) class are taught the language as well.*

Dei and his classmate enjoy using the computer to learn English.

Sometimes the students spend a whole class learning about a single letter of the alphabet. When the teacher asks if the children know any words that start with the letter *s*, Dei raises his hand. The teacher calls on him. "Snake!" he says proudly. A boy who speaks Spanish then says "Zebra!" taking Dei's lead in using animal names. The teacher explains that while a *z* sounds like an *s* in Spanish, it sounds different in English.

Then the students draw pictures of things that start with the letter *s*. Dei sketches a man surrounded by large snowflakes, since snow is falling outside. Dei has never seen snow before, and as the flakes fall, he keeps looking out the window. Finally, the teacher lets everyone go to the door to see the heavy clumps of white that are covering the grass.

Back in the main classroom, Dei continues to practice his English. He often sits and works at the computer stations with the help of other students. Sometimes Dei selects a computer program that shows a person working at a job. He then learns new words related to the pictures and the story that goes with them. Dei uses headphones with the computer, so he can hear all the special sounds that go with the program and learn the correct way of pronouncing the words. Although Dei listens to the words, he usually doesn't repeat them out loud. He laughs a lot, because the program has funny pictures and sounds.

Dei also gets special help with English from the teacher's aide, who works alone with him for a little while each day. She asks him to repeat words and letters that are written on cards.

One of Dei's favorite subjects in school is math, and he often raises his hand to answer the teacher's questions on addition, subtraction, multiplication, and division. Because he is not yet comfortable speaking English, he replies quietly, with one-word answers.

"How much is twelve plus six?" asks Ms. Burrell, as the students sit in a group on the carpeted floor. Dei's hand goes up quickly. "Eighteen," he says softly. "Correct," agrees Ms. Burrell.

"Now if Dei Dei's mother takes him to the store and gives him twenty-five cents, and Dei Dei buys some candy for fifteen cents, how much money does he have left?" Dei smiles broadly at this question but doesn't offer an answer. The other children respond in his place.

Dei enjoys looking at the books that are available in the classroom, even though it's hard for him to read English. "He loves the books," Jock says. Dei also likes to study science. "Because he likes animals," his father explains.

Dei gets help from the teacher's aid to learn the English alphabet.

When the teacher asks a math question, Dei is one of the first to raise his hand with an answer.

(Left) *A group of Dei's friends meets in the school yard to play.* (Below) *Dei eats lunch with his classmates.*

Dei may be very quiet in the classroom, but he watches everything and smiles a lot as he begins to understand English. He eats lunch in the school cafeteria, where he learns more and more about American food. Dei tries many of the new dishes served at school and usually finishes them. One day the meal consists of a hamburger, collard greens, beans, milk, and applesauce. Dei cleans his plate, sitting at a long table with the rest of his class. Everyone talks to each other during lunch—about the food, about birthday parties and birthday cakes, about places they have lived. Although Dei seems to enjoy the time with his friends, he doesn't speak. He just nods his head and smiles.

Dei's classmates are friendly. All day long students help Dei, watching out for him and his belongings. "That's Dei Dei's coat," says one of the girls when someone finds a jacket on the floor. "Dei Dei *walks* home!" says another, when Dei accidentally joins the line for those who take the bus.

Dei's teammates cheer for him on the playing field, where his long legs and quick reflexes help him excel at soccer.

Dei always looks forward to Friday's physical education class, when the students play soccer. In the Kenyan refugee camps, soccer was a popular sport among the boys. Because he is tall and quick, Dei is one of the best soccer players in his class. The students and teachers encourage him. Everyone shouts when Dei kicks the ball. They yell, "Here, Dei Dei!" as he prepares to throw the ball back onto the field.

After school Dei has some other favorite activities. He received a bicycle from some of the church members and enjoys riding it around the apartment complex and on the nearby sidewalks. He also has a small electric piano keyboard and likes to make music. Sometimes Kong comes down from upstairs to join in. The piano can play chords, rhythms, and even entire songs all by itself, so the boys can make a lot of noise. Whenever someone comes to visit the apartment, Dei turns on the instrument and pushes some buttons so that it will play a song very loudly. Then he giggles.

"It's funny," says Dei, smiling beside the piano.

Dei's family is very welcoming to visitors and new friends who come to the apartment. His mother, Nyawal, has not learned much English, but one of her first words is "welcome."

Dei likes his new life, his apartment, and his school. Why? "They are good!" he exclaims. He's also fascinated by other new experiences, such as riding in a car. A big interstate highway runs near his apartment, and Dei has seen all the traffic. When a friend comes to the apartment in a car, Dei asks excitedly, "We go in the car?"

Making music keeps Dei (top) busy. (Right) Dei makes friends with the members of his soccer team.

(Below, clockwise from left) *Jock, Dei, and Pal recognized familiar animals from Africa, such as lions* (right), *at the zoo in Atlanta.* (Above) *Pal was most interested in the gorillas.*

One day Dei, Jock, Pal, and Nyachan take a trip to the local zoo with some American friends. Dei is excited because he wants to see the animals he remembers from Africa. "Can we see lions?" he asks several times on the way. Little Pal, who is only two years old and just beginning to talk, is fascinated by a family of gorillas in a grassy, outdoor exhibit.

"Do they have blood?" Pal asks his father in Nuer. Jock explains proudly, "He wants to know if they are toys, or if they are real. This is a very smart boy."

Dei remembers little about Sudan, but he recalls the fighting and living in wooden huts. He also has only sketchy ideas about Nuer culture and traditions, since he is so young and has moved around so often. His father hopes that at least some of their beliefs can be preserved in the future, but he worries because there are so few Sudanese people nearby.

One very special Nuer tradition involves face markings. When Nuer boys reach the age of about 14 to 17 they have special markings cut into their faces. These marks are made using needles and razor blades. The cuts, which are arranged into a neat pattern, form small, round scars—or bumps—on the face.

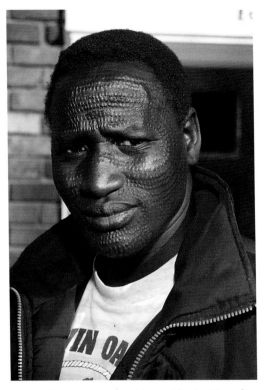

"The marks on the upper part of the face show that you have become a man," explains Jock. Another kind of mark is made for beauty. Men and women both have these marks. The procedure for making marks can be dangerous and painful. People are specially trained to make face markings for others. Dei's mother and father both have markings on their faces. Dei's father hopes Dei will want face markings in a few years when he comes of age.

The Nuer people have a unique and very democratic way of ruling themselves. Each year certain members of the community go to a special place to settle disputes that the people haven't been able to solve on

Dei will choose for himself whether he receives the special Nuer markings on his face (above). *The family dinner* (right) *is a good place to gather and talk at the end of the day.*

their own. They discuss the problems until they find a solution. Dei's father feels it is important to have the family work in a similar way. Each person must have the freedom to make decisions on his or her own and must not be forced by the others to do anything he or she doesn't want to do. Although Jock would like Dei to continue Nuer traditions and to follow the ways of the Seventh Day Adventist Church, the decision will always be up to Dei.

In the meantime, on Saturdays Jock invites the few other Nuer people in Atlanta to come and sit in his living room. They discuss life in the United States and ways they can help those still remaining in the refugee camps. "I want to find out how I can send clothing to them," says Jock one Saturday. "It is too expensive to use the post office. They need the clothing."

Dei arrives home after a day at school.

The Nuer have rich traditions of song, dance, and storytelling. Nuer folktales fall under four main subjects: the origins of their people; animals; ogres (monsters); and clever riddles about the world around them. "The Words of a Man," told below, is an animal tale that reflects the importance of cattle to the Nuer as well as the democratic decision-making process of the village.

A man met a snake one day. The snake gave him a charm saying, "With this charm, you will hear all things. When the rat talks, you will hear it. When the cow talks, you will hear it. You will hear everything that is said." The man left and went back to his village.

At night the man's wife locked up their house tightly. It was quite dark. She and her husband lay down to sleep. A mosquito came to the door. It examined the house and found no way in. The mosquito exclaimed, "They have locked the house very tightly. How can I get in?" The man understood and laughed. "What are you laughing about?" asked the wife. "Nothing," he said.

A rat came. He examined the door. He found it closed and tried the eaves of the house. He got in. Searching everywhere, he looked for butter to eat but found none. He said, "Where has that woman stored her butter?" The man laughed. His wife asked him, "What are you laughing about?" He answered, "Nothing."

In the morning, the man went to his barn. He let the cattle out. When it was milking time, his wife came to the barn. The cow said, "Of course you come, but you will not milk me today. I will keep my milk. My calf will drink it." The man laughed. His wife asked him, "What are you laughing at?" He answered, "Nothing."

The wife left the cow after trying unsuccessfully to get milk. She returned to the village. The calf drank its mother's milk.

The next day the wife came again to milk. Again, the cow withheld its milk. In the afternoon the woman's child became ill from having no milk. The mother brought her child to the barn. She talked to her husband. She said, "That calf will kill my daughter." The cow interrupted, "What! My daughter will kill your daughter?" The man laughed. His wife asked him, "What are you laughing about?" He answered, "Nothing."

When it was nearly sunset his wife said, "I will get a divorce." She called all the people to the large village tree, where important decisions were made. They said to the wife, "You and your husband talk. We will listen." The wife talked. She said to the people, "When we lie down to sleep, my husband always laughs at me without any reason. When I ask him why he does it, he hides the reason from me. That is why I object to him."

Then they asked the husband, "Why do you laugh at your wife? Tell us." He answered, "Men, if I tell it, I will die." They said, "Tell it, man. Do not hide it." He replied, "Oh, men, I will not tell. I will surely die." They urged him. When he was worn out, he told them about the snake's charm and about hearing the animals speak. The man died, as he had predicted. The people cried. Some of them dug a grave. As they were about to bury the body, a certain snake hurried to the spot and revived the man.

When the man had recovered, he went to the spot where he had first seen the snake. He found the snake under a tree. The snake said, "Why did you tell? Long ago when I gave you that charm, I told you it would make you hear all things." The man replied, "They urged me, so I told them." The snake said, "Oh!" Then the snake gave him another charm saying, "You will hear the words of the birds that eat the corn."

The snake went away. The man returned to the village. He heard many things. When a bird was eating the corn, if another bird came near, the first one would say, "Bird, do not come. We will be seen. I am eating quietly. This is my place. Let's separate. The field is large." The man laughed there in the corn, but he did not tell the villagers what he had heard. And the people did not ask.

This story is reprinted, with minor adaptations, from Ray Huffman's Nuer Customs and Folklore *(Oxford University Press for the International African Institute, 1931).*

The Nuer people's democratic philosophy also extends to marriage. Young people choose whom they wish to marry, but their families must agree on some of the details. For example, the father of the groom must pay the father of the bride, using such possessions as cows. "So it is very expensive if you have a lot of sons," explains Jock. Jock hopes that his children will be able to meet other Nuer young people to marry. This dream could happen if more Sudanese are allowed to immigrate to the United States from Africa.

Another Nuer tradition concerns how individuals are named. When a man and a woman marry, the wife does not take her husband's name. This is a way of bringing families together without ignoring the woman's family name. When a child is born, the father and mother choose a first name for the baby. The second name is that of the child's father. The third, or last, name is the name of the child's paternal grandfather. Nobody calls another person by his or her last name. Instead, the first two names are used. So, in the Nuer tradition, Dei's name is Dei Jock, meaning Dei, son of Jock.

In his new home in the United States, Dei (above) has the freedom to decide his own future. (Left) Dei and Nyachan share a bedroom.

Jock fears that Pal will have a hard time learning about Nuer traditions because he left Africa at such a young age. "I think maybe I will not send Pal to school, so that he can stay home and learn about Nuer culture," he says. Dei and Nyachan, who are attending school, have already become very Americanized. Nyachan likes to wear bright dresses and skirts, and Dei looks like an all-American kid in his blue jeans and sneakers.

Dei's parents read the Bible and pray every day. "We pray extra for the famine in Africa, for the people dying there, for the government," notes Jock. *Male,* the Nuer term for "peace," is one word the family thinks of often. They hope that other Nuer people will be able to join them soon in the United States. In the meantime, Jock hopes to send clothing and money back to Africa. He knows how desperate the situation is there.

Jock says the family could not return to Sudan and be safe, although perhaps one day this situation will change. "It is very dangerous, very dangerous," he says. The future of the government in Sudan is uncertain. Jock believes that perhaps one day the country will divide into two separate parts—the north and the south. No one really knows what will happen. "Freedom is everything," says Jock. "The world is freedom." Sadly, though, not even Jock, who is in his thirties, remembers a time when Sudan was not at war.

The Sudanese continue to face hard times in Africa.

Dei is unsure what his future holds, but his friends and family will help him.

 For the time being, the United States is the safest place for Dei's family to live. Here Jock hopes to complete his college education while also working to support his family. He has been frustrated with his job opportunities in Atlanta because he cannot earn enough money to pay for much more than rent and food. This situation makes attending college impossible. So Jock has been looking for other places in the United States where he might be able to do both.

From talking to the other Sudanese refugees in Atlanta, Jock discovered that many Sudanese people live in San Diego, California. Jock quickly made plans to move the family there. He spent most of the money he had earned to buy one-way bus tickets. The family packed their clothes and other belongings in cardboard boxes and a few suitcases. They left their donated furniture behind in the apartment.

Jock hopes to be able to attend a church college near San Diego. Eventually, he dreams of working for a church or some other group that helps people—either in the United States or in Africa.

Dei says he does not know how far it is to California, even though he can find the state on his wall map. "It will take two days on the bus," a friend tells him as they leave for the bus station. Dei looks amazed. "Two days?" he asks with surprise.

In June 1995, a year from their arrival in the United States, Dei Jock Dei and his family boarded the Greyhound bus in Atlanta to begin another long trip. They took with them some milk, a bag of hard-boiled eggs, and $100 given to them by a friend, for food on the trip. Dei would have to make new friends again, but more importantly, he and his family would be safe. In their new home in San Diego, they would continue to follow their goals and dreams rather than running from war and famine. In San Diego they hoped to finally find *male*—or peace.

San Diego, California, holds many unknown opportunities for Jock, Nyawal, Nyachan, Dei, and Pal.

FURTHER READING

Aardema, Verna. *What's So Funny, Ketu?: A Nuer Tale.* New York: Dial Press, 1982.

Cultures of the World: Sudan. North Bellmore, New York: Marshall Cavendish, 1996.

Mitchnik, Helen. *Egyptian and Sudanese Folktales.* Oxford, England: Oxford University Press, 1978.

Roddis, Ingrid and Miles. *Let's Visit Sudan.* London: Burke Publishing, 1985.

Sudan in Pictures. Minneapolis: Lerner Publications Company, 1988.

Stewart, Judy. *A Family in Sudan.* Minneapolis: Lerner Publications Company, 1988.

Wilkes, Sybella. *One Day We Had to Run!* Brookfield, Connecticut: The Millbrook Press, 1994.

PRONUNCIATION GUIDE

Dei (DAYEE)
Dinka (DIHNG-kuh)
dra (DRAH)
Jock (JAHK)
Khartoum (kahr-TOOM)
Kong (KAHNG)
male (MAHL)
Nilotic (ny-LAH-teek)
Nubia (NOO-bee-uh)
Nuer (NOO-uhr)
Nyachan (ny-SHAHN)
Nyawal (ny-WAHL)
Pal (PAHL)

*The sounds of the languages of Africa are often difficult to translate into English. The pronunciations on this page are approximations.

INDEX

ABOUT THE AUTHOR

Erika F. Archibald, a former journalist, received her Ph.D. in journalism from the University of Georgia. She is a freelance writer, as well as a teacher of journalism and of writing courses at North Georgia College in Atlanta. She has also worked as the public relations and marketing director of the Atlanta Zoo, where she indulged her love of animals. Originally from New York, she lives in Atlanta and is an enthusiastic traveler.

PHOTO ACKNOWLEDGMENTS

Cover photographs by Kay Chernush/Agency for International Development (left) and Erika Archibald (right). All inside photos by Erika Archibald and Greg Nelson except the following: Kay Chernush/Agency for International Development, p. 6; CARE pp. 7, 23, 51; Jenny Matthews from *A Family in Sudan* by Judy Stewart (A & C Black), pp. 8, 17 (bottom); Agency for International Development, pp. 9, 21 (right); © Liba Taylor/Panos Pictures, p. 14 (top); Courtesy of Kenneth J. Perkins, p. 14 (bottom), 21 (left); © Betty Press/Panos Pictures, pp. 16, 17 (top); Archive Photos, p. 19; © Crispin Hughs/Panos Pictures, p. 20; Bettmann, p. 22 (top); Carolyn Gorman, U.S. Department of State, Bureau of Population, Refugees, and Migration, pp. 22 (bottom), 24 (left); Courtesy of Lutheran Immigration and Refugee Service, p. 24 (right); Nancy Smedstad, p. 25 (both); © J. Hartley/Panos Pictures, p. 29 (top); Atlanta Convention and Visitors Bureau, p.35; UPI/Corbis-Bettmann, p. 36; Courtesy of Zoo Atlanta, p. 44 (top and right); © James Blank, p. 53; pottery cut-ins, detail from Nubian jar, by Fitzwilliam Museum, Cambridge. All artwork and maps by Laura Westlund.